Questions and Answers
SCIENCE

Questions and Answers

SCIENCE

chris oxlade

Miles
KeLLy

First published in 2014 by Miles Kelly Publishing Ltd
Harding's Barn, Bardfield End Green, Thaxted, Essex, CM6 3PX, UK

2 4 6 8 10 9 7 5 3 1

Publishing Director Belinda Gallagher
Creative Director Jo Cowan
Editors Amanda Askew, Lucy Dowling
Designers Jo Cowan, Sally Lace, Joe Jones, Elaine Wilkinson
Cover Designer Rob Hale
Production Manager Elizabeth Collins
Reprographics Stephan Davis, Jennifer Hunt, Thom Allaway

ISBN 978-1-78209-473-9

Printed in China

British Library Cataloguing-in-Publication Data
A catalogue record for this book is available from the British Library

ACKNOWLEDGEMENTS

The publishers would like to thank the following for the use of their photograph:
Cover Triff/Shutterstock.com

Made with paper from a sustainable forest
www.mileskelly.net   info@mileskelly.net

Contents

Is science in the playground?

Yes, it is! Lots of science happens in a playground. The playground rides could not work without science. A see-saw is a simple machine called a lever. It has a long arm and a point in the middle called a pivot. As you ride on the see-saw, the lever tips up and down on the pivot.

See-saw

Lever

Pivot

Sloping machine!

A ramp is the simplest machine of all. It is easier to walk up a ramp to the top of a hill than it is to climb a steep hillside.

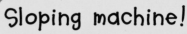

What is a wheel?

A wheel is a very simple machine that can spin around. Wheels let other machines, such as skateboards, bicycles, cars and trains, roll along smoothly. They also make it easy to move heavy weights in carts and wheelbarrows.

Feel

Press the palm of your hand onto a table. A force called friction stops you sliding your hand along.

What makes things stop and start?

Pushes and pulls make things stop and start. Scientists use the word 'force' for pushes and pulls. Forces are all around us. The force of gravity pulls things downwards. It makes a rollercoaster car hurtle downhill. It also slows the car on the uphill parts of the track.

Rollercoaster

Why do fireworks flash and bang?

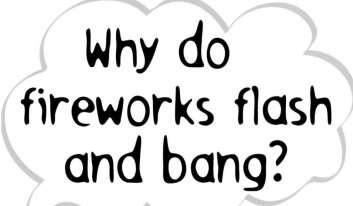

Fireworks flash and bang because they are full of chemicals that burn. The chemicals have lots of energy stored in them. When they burn, the energy changes to light, heat and sound. We use chemicals that burn in other places too, such as cookers, heaters and car engines.

Fireworks

How do candles burn?

Candles are made of wax and a wick (string). When the wick is lit, the wax around it melts. The wick then soaks up the liquid wax and the heat of the flame turns the wax into a gas (vapour), which burns away. As the wax becomes vapour it cools the wick, allowing the candle to burn slowly.

Hot! Hot! Hot!

The hottest-ever temperature recorded was in a science laboratory. It was four hundred million degrees Celsius (400,000,000°C).

What is a thermometer?

A thermometer tells us how hot something is. This is called temperature. The numbers written on a thermometer are normally degrees Celsius (°C). If you put a thermometer in cold water, it shows 0°C. If you put it in boiling water it shows 100°C. A thermometer can also measure your body temperature.

Remember

Which piece of equipment is used to measure how hot or cold something is?

What is in an electric motor?

Magnets and wires. Electricity from a battery passes through the wires. This turns the wires into a magnet. Two more magnets on each side of the motor push and pull against the wires. This makes a thin metal rod (spindle) spin around.

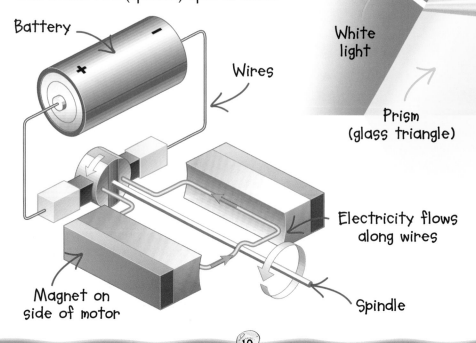

Battery

Wires

White light

Prism (glass triangle)

Electricity flows along wires

Magnet on side of motor

Spindle

10

Why does light bend?

Light rays travel in straight lines. When light shines through a prism, the rays bend because light travels more slowly through glass than air. Sunlight is called white light, but it is made up of a mixture of colours. When white light passes through a prism it splits into many colours, like a rainbow.

Fast as light!

Light is the fastest thing in the Universe. It travels 300,000 kilometres every second. That means it could travel around the Earth seven times in less than a second!

Rainbow colours

Make

On a sunny day, stand with your back to the Sun. Spray water into the air and you should see a rainbow!

What is the loudest sound?

The roar of a jet engine is the loudest sound we normally hear. It is thousands of times louder than someone shouting. Sounds this loud can damage our ears if we are too close to them. The quietest sounds we can hear are things like rustling leaves.

Where is science in a city?

Everywhere! In a big city, almost every machine, building and vehicle is based on science. Cars, buses and trains help us move around the city. Scientists and engineers have also worked out how to build tall skyscrapers where people live and work.

City

Look

Look at the city picture. How many different forms of transport can you see?

12

Railway signals

Who works railway signals?

Nobody does! The signals work by themselves. Electronic parts on the track work out if a train is passing. Then a computer changes the signals to red, to stop another train moving onto the same piece of track.

How do skyscrapers stay up?

Skyscrapers stay up because they have a strong frame on the inside. The frame is made from steel and concrete. These are very strong materials. Normally you can't see the frame. It is hidden by the skyscraper's walls. The walls hang on the frame.

Plane spotters!

There's science at an airport, too. A radar machine uses radio waves to find aircraft in the sky. This helps people at the airport to guide the aircraft onto the runway.

How do you make magnets?

By using another magnet! Magnets are made from lumps of iron or steel. You can turn a piece of iron into a magnet by stroking it with another magnet. A magnet can also be made by sending electricity through a coil of wire. This is called an electromagnet. Some electromagnets are so strong, they can pick up cars.

Electromagnet picking up scrap cars

Count

Find a magnet at home (you can use a fridge magnet). How many paper clips can your magnet pick up?

Does a magnet have a field?

Yes – but it's not a field of grass! The area around a magnet is called a magnetic field. A magnetic field is shown by drawing lines around a magnet. The Earth has a magnetic field, too. It is as though there is a giant magnet inside the Earth.

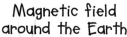

Magnetic field around the Earth

What are poles?

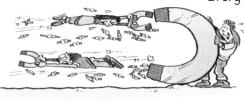

Every magnet has two poles. These are where the pull of a magnet is strongest. They are called the north pole and the south pole. A north pole and a south pole always pull towards each other. Two north poles always push each other away. So do two south poles.

Handy rock!

Some rocks act like magnets. Years ago, people used magnetic rocks to find their way. If they let the rock spin round, it always pointed in the same direction.

Where does electricity come from?

Battery

Electricity comes to your home along cables from power stations. The cables are held off the ground by pylons. Around your home are holes in the wall called sockets. When a machine is plugged into a socket, electricity flows out to work the machine.

Electric!

Our homes are full of machines that work using electricity. If there was no electricity we wouldn't have televisions, lights, washing machines or computers!

Power station

Remember

Mains electricity is very dangerous. It could kill you. Never play with mains sockets in your home.

Light bulb

Switch

What is a circuit?

A circuit is a loop that electricity moves around. This circuit is made up of a battery, a light bulb and a switch. If the switch is turned off, the loop would be broken. Then the electricity would stop moving and the light would go out.

When is electricity in the sky?

When there's a thunderstorm! During a storm, a kind of electricity called static electricity builds up. This can make a big flash, that lights up the sky. This is lightning. The hot lightning heats up the air around it and this makes a loud clap. This is thunder.

Pylon holds cables off the ground

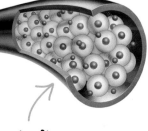

Electricity flows along the cables

What waves are invisible?

Radio waves are all around us, but we can't see them. We use radio waves to send sounds and pictures to radios and televisions. Some radio waves come from satellites in space. A radio set receives radio waves through a metal rod called an aerial. A dish-shaped aerial picks up radio waves for television programmes.

Satellite

Radio waves

Aerial

Radio

Remember
Which part of your body would stop an X-ray? Skin or bone?

X-ray
machine

What is an X-ray?

An X-ray is like a radio wave. X-rays can go through the soft bits of your body. However, hard bones stop them. That's why doctors use X-ray machines to take pictures of the inside of people's bodies.

Picture
of bone

Space radio!

Radio waves can travel through space. But they can't travel through water. So you can listen to a radio in a space station, but not in a submarine!

Dish-shaped
aerial

What waves can cook food?

Microwaves can. These are a kind of radio wave. They have lots of energy in them. A microwave uses this energy to cook food. Microwaves are fired into the oven. They make the particles in the food jiggle about. This makes the food hot.

Are computers clever?

Not really! Computers are amazing machines, but they can only do what they are told. They carry out computer programs written down by people. These are full of instructions that the computer follows. You can also tell a computer what to do by using its keyboard and mouse.

Typing on a keyboard

Mouse

Remember

Can you remember the name for a computer's electronic brain? Read these pages again to help you.

Microchip

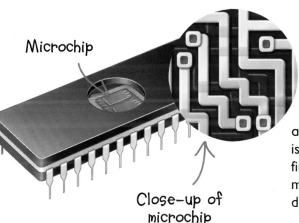

Close-up of
microchip

Does a computer have a brain?

A computer doesn't have a brain like yours. It has an electronic brain called a central processing unit. This is a microchip the size of your fingernail. This amazing mini machine can do millions of difficult sums in a split second.

Computer

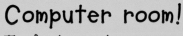

Computer room!

The first computer was made 60 years ago. It was so big that it filled a whole room. A modern calculator can do sums much more quickly!

How does a computer remember?

A computer remembers with its electronic memory. This is made up of lots of tiny microchips. When you turn the computer off, everything in the memory is lost. So you have to save your work on a disc, otherwise you lose it when you switch off.

Is the Internet like a web?

 **The Internet is made up of millions of computers around the world.** They are connected like a giant spider's web! A computer connects to a machine called a modem. This sends signals to a server. The server lets you connect to the Internet. People can send emails and open web pages.

Modem

Email

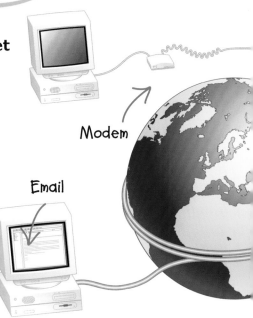

Find out

Look at the main picture on these pages. See if you can find out what the word 'email' is short for.

What does www stand for?

The letters www are short for World Wide Web. The World Wide Web is like a giant library of information, stored on computers all over the world. There are also thousands of shops on the World Wide Web, where you can buy almost anything.

Can I use the Internet without a computer?

Yes. Other machines can link to the Internet, too. You can see simple information from the Internet on a mobile phone. You can send and get emails, too. A mobile phone connects to the Internet by radio.

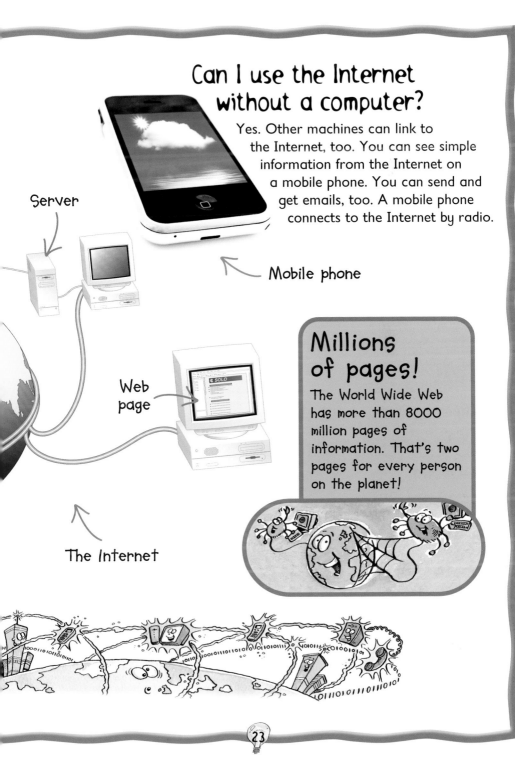

Server

Mobile phone

Web page

Millions of pages!

The World Wide Web has more than 8000 million pages of information. That's two pages for every person on the planet!

The Internet

Can a car be made from card?

Yes, it can – but it would break if you sat inside it! It is always important to use the right material to make something. Cars are made from tough, long-lasting materials. Metal, plastic and rubber are all materials used to make cars.

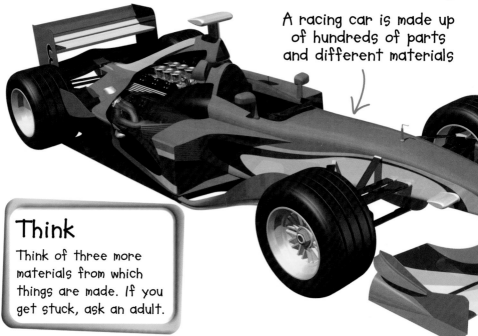

A racing car is made up of hundreds of parts and different materials

Think

Think of three more materials from which things are made. If you get stuck, ask an adult.

Cotton plants make clothes

What materials grow?

Many of the materials we use every day come from plants. Wood comes from the trunks and branches of trees. Cotton is made from the seeds of cotton plants to make clothes such as T-shirts. Some rubber is made from a liquid (sap) from rubber trees.

Rubber tree makes tyres

Tree trunks and branches make wooden bats

Does glass grow?

Glass doesn't grow! It is made from sand and two other materials called limestone and soda. These materials are mixed together and melted to make a gooey liquid. When the mixture cools down, it forms the hard glass that we use to make windows, drinking glasses and other objects.

Bullet proof!

Some glass is extra-strong. Toughened glass is so hard that even a bullet from a gun bounces off it!

What do scientists do at work?

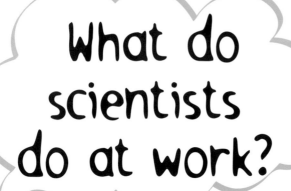

Some scientists try to find out about the world around us. Others find out about space, planets and stars. Some scientists discover useful materials that we can use. Scientists carry out experiments in laboratories to test their ideas.

Scientist in a laboratory

Who is the most famous scientist?

The most famous scientist is called Albert Einstein (1879–1955). He made many discoveries about time, space, the force of gravity and nuclear energy. The ideas that Einstein wrote down were so amazing that they made him famous across the world.

Albert Einstein

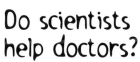

Atom pie!

One hundred years ago, scientists thought that the pieces in an atom were all spread out, like the raisins in a pudding. Now we know they are all bunched together.

Do scientists help doctors?

Yes, they do. Many scientists make medicines that the doctor gives you when you are ill. They also help to make the complicated machines that doctors use in hospitals. Scientists also try to find out what makes us ill, and how we can stay healthy.

Find

Find out the name of the country where Albert Einstein was born. An encyclopedia will help you.

27

Why do babies grip so tightly?

Tiny babies can do simple things. If something touches a baby's cheek, it turns its head and tries to suck. If something touches the baby's hand, it grips tightly. These actions are called reflexes. They help the baby survive.

Giant baby!

A baby grows quickly before it is born. If it grew this fast for 50 years, it would be taller than Mount Everest!

Baby gripping

When do babies start to walk?

When they are about one year old. Babies can roll over at three months. At six months, they can sit up. At nine months they start to crawl. Then babies learn to stand and take their first steps.

Children playing

Am I always learning?

Yes, you are! Most children start school when they are five years old. They learn to count, read, write and draw. Children learn outside of the classroom, too. Playing and having fun with friends is a great way to learn new things!

Find out

Find out three reasons why a newborn baby cries? Ask a grown-up if you need any help.

What does my skin do?

Skin protects you from bumps and scratches. It stops your body from drying out, and prevents germs from getting in. When you play on bikes or skateboards, you should wear gloves and knee pads to protect your skin.

Knee pads protect from cuts

Gloves protect from scrapes

Ouch! Ouch! Ouch!

There are millions of tiny touch sensors in your skin. They tell your brain when something touches your skin. Some sensors feel hot and cold. Others feel pain. Ouch!

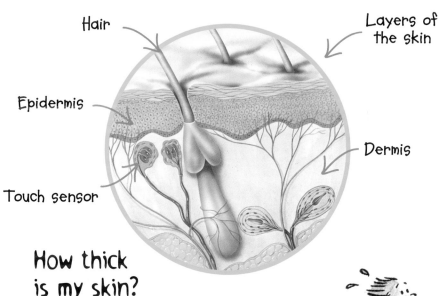

Hair

Layers of the skin

Epidermis

Dermis

Touch sensor

How thick is my skin?

Your skin is very thin. It is only 2 millimetres thick. On top is a layer of tough, dead cells called the epidermis. These cells gradually rub off. New cells grow underneath to replace them. Underneath is another layer of skin called the dermis. This contains areas that give you your sense of touch.

Think

If you are riding a bike or playing on a skateboard, what should you wear on your head, and why?

Why do I sweat when I'm warm?

To cool down again. Your body warms up on a hot day or when you run about. You sweat to get rid of the heat. Your body lets sweat out through your skin. As the sweat dries, it takes away heat. This cools you down.

How much hair do I have?

Your whole body is covered in about five million hairs! You have about 100,000 hairs on your head. Hair grows out of tiny pits in your skin, called follicles. Hair grows in different colours and it can be wavy, curly or straight.

Blonde wavy hair

Red straight hair

Black straight hair

Black curly hair

For the chop!

The hair on your head grows about 2 millimetres a week. If a hair is never cut, it reaches about one metre in length before it falls out. It is replaced by a new hair.

What are nails made from?

Fingernails and toenails are made from a hard material called keratin. It is the same material that hair is made from. Nails grow out of the nail root. In a week, a nail grows by about half a millimetre. They grow faster at night than in the day!

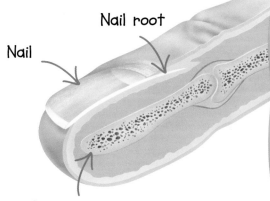

Nail root

Nail

Finger bone

Look

Have a look in the mirror. Is your hair straight, wavy or curly? Use the pictures on page 32 to help you.

Why do we have fingernails?

Fingernails protect your fingertips. The nail stops your fingertip bending back when you touch something. This helps your fingers to feel things. Nails are useful for picking up tiny objects.

How many bones do I have?

Most people have 206 bones. Half of them are in your hands and feet. All your bones together make up your skeleton. The skeleton is like a frame. It holds up the other parts of your body. It also protects the squashy bits inside.

Find

Can you find your collarbone? It starts at your shoulder and runs to the top of your rib cage.

Skeleton key

1. Skull
2. Collar bone
3. Shoulder blade
4. Ribs
5. Upper arm bone
6. Pelvis
7. Thigh bone
8. Kneecap
9. Calf bone
10. Shin bone

What are bones made from?

Bones are made from different materials mixed together. Some of the materials are very hard and some are tough and bendy. Together they make bones very strong. There is a kind of jelly called marrow inside some bones. This makes tiny parts for your blood, called red and white cells.

Marrow

Hard bone

Spongy bone

Strong bones!

Your bone is lightweight but super-strong. It is stronger than concrete or steel, which are used for making buildings and bridges! But bones can still break if they are bent too much.

How are bones joined together?

Your bones are connected by joints. They let your back, arms, legs, fingers and toes move. You have about 100 joints. The largest joints are in your hips and knees. The smallest joints are inside your ear.

How do muscles work?

Muscles are made from fibres that look like bits of string. The fibres get shorter to make the muscle pull. The biggest muscles in your body are the ones that you sit on – your bottom! You use them when you walk and run. The strongest muscle in your body is in your jaw.

Muscle fibre

Nerve

Why do knees bend?

Muscles make your joints, such as your knees, bend. They help you to run, jump, hold and lift things. In fact you need muscles to move all of your body parts.

Cheeky muscles!

Your face is full of muscles. You use them to smile, to wrinkle your nose, or to cry. You use more muscles to frown than to smile!

What makes my muscles move?

Your brain does. It sends messages along nerves to your muscles. Lots of muscles are needed, even for small movements, like writing with a pen. Your brain controls other muscles without you thinking about it. For example, the muscles in your heart keep working even when you are asleep.

Muscle

Feel

Bend and unbend your arm. Can you feel your arm muscles getting shorter and longer?

37

Why do I need to breathe?

You breathe to take air into your body. There is a gas in the air called oxygen that your body needs to work. The air goes up your nose or into your mouth. Then it goes down a tube called the windpipe and into your lungs.

1. Air goes into your nose or mouth

2. Air goes down the windpipe

3. Air enters the lungs

Count
How many times do you breathe in and out in one minute?

Is my voice kept in a box?

Not quite! The real name for your voicebox is the larynx. It's at the top of the windpipe, and makes a bulge at the front of your neck. Air passing through the voicebox makes it shake, or vibrate. This is the sound of your voice. Your voice can make lots of sounds, and helps you to sing!

Singing

What makes air go into my lungs?

There is a big muscle under your lungs that moves down. More muscles make your ribs move out. This makes your lungs bigger. Air rushes into your lungs to fill the space. When your muscles relax, the air is pushed out again.

Fill 'em up!

When you are resting, you take in enough air to fill a can of fizzy drink in every breath. When you are running, you breathe in ten times as much air.

What are teeth made of?

Teeth are covered in a material called enamel. This is harder than most kinds of rock! Teeth are fixed into your jaw bones by roots. Sharp front teeth (incisors) bite food into small pieces. Tall, pointy teeth (canines) tear and pull food. Flat back teeth (molars) chew food to a mush.

Canine

Incisor

Molar

Root

How many sets of teeth do I have?

You have two sets. A baby is born without teeth. The first set of teeth appears when a child is six months old. This set has 20 teeth. These teeth fall out at about seven years old. They are replaced by 32 adult teeth.

Discover
Do you still have your first set of teeth, or have your baby teeth begun to fall out?

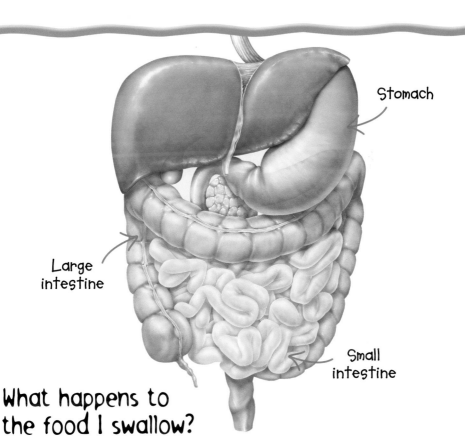

Stomach

Large
intestine

Small
intestine

What happens to the food I swallow?

The food you swallow goes into your stomach. Here, special juices and strong muscles break the food up into a thick mush. The mushy food then goes into a long tube called the intestines. Here, all the goodness from the food is taken out, to be used by our body.

All gone!

When you go to the toilet, you get rid of waste. This is leftover food. It is stored in your large intestine until you go to the toilet.

Why does my heart beat?

To pump blood and oxygen around your body. Your heart is about the size of your fist and is made of muscle. When it beats, your heart squeezes blood into tubes. These carry blood and oxygen around your body. The blood then comes back to the heart from the lungs, with more oxygen.

Blood to body

Blood from body

Blood to lungs

Blood from lung

Blood from lung

Heart muscles

Blood from body

Blood to body

Beat of life!

Your heart beats once a second for the whole of your life. That is 86,000 beats a day, and 31 million beats a year. In total, this is 2000 million beats in your life.

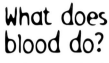

What does blood do?

Your whole body needs oxygen to work. Blood carries oxygen to every part of your body in its red cells. Blood also contains white cells that fight germs. Tubes called arteries and veins carry blood around your body.

Artery

Red cell

Does blood get dirty?

Yes, it does. Because blood carries waste away from your body parts, it has to be cleaned. This is done by your kidneys. They take the waste out of the blood and make a liquid called urine. This liquid leaves your body when you go to the toilet.

White cell

Feel

Touch your neck under your chin. Can you feel the blood flowing through an artery to your brain?

Are my eyes like a camera?

Your eyes work like a tiny camera. They collect light that bounces off the things you are looking at. This makes tiny pictures at the back of the eyes. Here, millions of sensors pick up the light. They send a picture to your brain along a nerve.

In a spin!

Inside your ear are loops full of liquid. They can tell when you move your head. This helps you to balance. If you spin around, the fluid keeps moving. This makes you feel dizzy!

Lens collects light

Pupil lets light into your eye

Nerve to brain

Muscles make eye move

What is inside my ears?

The flap on your head is only part of your ear. The hole in your ear goes to a tiny piece of tight skin, called an eardrum. Sounds enter your ear and make the eardrum move in and out. Tiny bones pass these movements to the cochlea, which is shaped like a snail. This is filled with liquid.

Look

Look in the mirror at your eye. Can you see the dark pupil where light goes in?

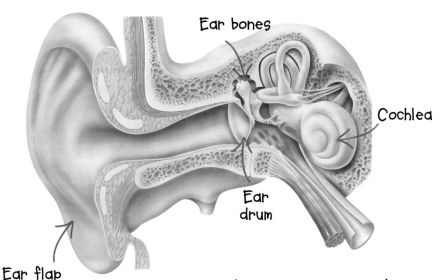

Ear bones

Cochlea

Ear drum

Ear flap

How do I hear sounds?

The cochlea in your ear contains thousands of tiny hairs. It is also is full of liquid. Sounds make the liquid move. This makes the hairs wave about. Tiny sensors pick up the waving, and send messages to your brain so you hear the sound.

Why can't I see smells?

Because they're invisible! Smells are tiny particles that float in the air. Inside the top of your nose are sticky smell sensors. When you sniff something, the sensors collect the smell particles. They send messages to your brain, which tell you what you can smell.

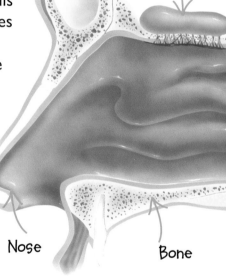

Smell sensors

Nose

Bone

A blocked dose!
Smell and taste work together when you eat. Your sense of smell helps you to taste flavours in food. When you have a cold, your smell sensors get blocked, so you cannot taste, either.

How do I taste things?

With your tongue. Your tongue is covered with tiny taste sensors. These are called taste buds. Buds on different parts of your tongue can sense different tastes, or flavours. Your tongue also moves food around your mouth and helps you to speak.

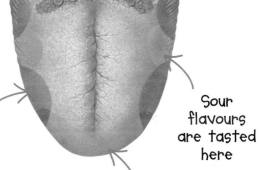

Salty flavours are tasted here

Sour flavours are tasted here

Sweet flavours are tasted here

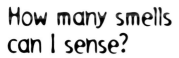

How many smells can I sense?

Your nose can sense about 3000 different smells. You don't just have a sense of smell so you can smell nice things, such as flowers and perfumes! Your sense of smell warns you if food is rotten before you eat it.

Think

Look at the picture of the tongue. Can you think of three different things that taste sour, sweet and salty?

47

Is my brain really big?

Your brain is about the same size as your two fists put together. It is the place where you think, remember, feel happy or sad – and dream. Your brain also takes information from your senses and controls your body. The main part is called the cerebrum.

Cerebrum

Right and left!

The main part of your brain is divided into two halves. The right half helps you to play music and to draw. The left half is good at thinking.

Cerebellum controls muscles

Brain stem

48

Can my brain really wave?

Well, sort of! Your brain works using electricity. It has about 10,000 million tiny nerve cells. Tiny bursts of electricity are always jumping around between the cells. Doctors can see your brain working by looking at the electricity with a special machine called an EEG. It shows the electricity as waves on a screen.

Remember

Your brain controls the five senses – smelling, tasting, touching, hearing – can you remember your fifth sense?

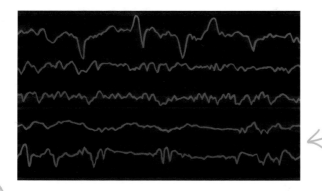

Brain waves from an EEG machine

How does my brain help me to play?

Different parts of your brain do different jobs. One part senses touch. Another part deals with thinking. Speaking is controlled by a different part. The cerebellum controls all your muscles. When you play and run, the cerebellum sends messages to your muscles to make them move.

Where did the Earth come from?

The Earth came from a cloud of dust. The dust whizzed around the Sun at speed and began to stick together to form lumps of rock. The rocks crashed into each other to make the planets. The Earth is one of these planets.

A cloud of dust spun around the Sun

Why does the Moon look lumpy?

Big rocks from space, called meteorites, have crashed into the Moon and made dents on its surface. These dents are called craters and they give the Moon a lumpy appearance.

Lumps of rock began to form

Look

At night, use some binoculars to look at the Moon. Can you see craters on its surface?

The Earth was formed from the lumps of rock →

What is the Earth made of?

The Earth is a huge ball-shaped lump of rock. Most of the Earth's surface is covered by water — this makes the seas and oceans. Rock that is not covered by water makes the land.

Face the Moon!

The Moon travels around the Earth. As the Moon doesn't spin, we only ever see one side of its surface.

51

Why does the Earth spin?

Morning

The Earth is always spinning.
This is because it was made
from a spinning cloud of gas
and dust. As it spins, the
Earth leans a little to one side.
It takes the Earth 24 hours to
spin around once. This
period of time is
called a day.

Evening

Discover
There are 24 hours
in a day. How many
minutes are there
in one hour?

Spinning Earth

52

Hot and cold!

In the Caribbean, the sea can be as warm as a bath. In the Arctic, it is so cold, that the sea freezes over.

Why do we have day and night?

Every day, each part of the Earth spins towards the Sun, and then away from it. When a part of the Earth is facing the Sun, it is daytime there. When that part is facing away from Earth, it is night time.

Mid-day

The Sun

Night

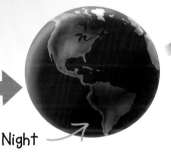

Do people live on the Moon?

No they don't. There is no air on the Moon so people cannot live there. Astronauts have visited the Moon in space rockets. They wear special equipment to help them breathe.

What is inside the Earth?

Crust

There are different layers inside the Earth. There is a thin, rocky crust, a solid area called the mantle and a centre called the core. The outer part of the core is made of hot, liquid metal. The inner core is made of solid metal.

Natural magnet!

Near the centre of the Earth is hot, liquid iron. As the Earth spins, the iron behaves like a magnet. This is why a compass needle points to North and South.

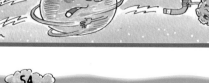

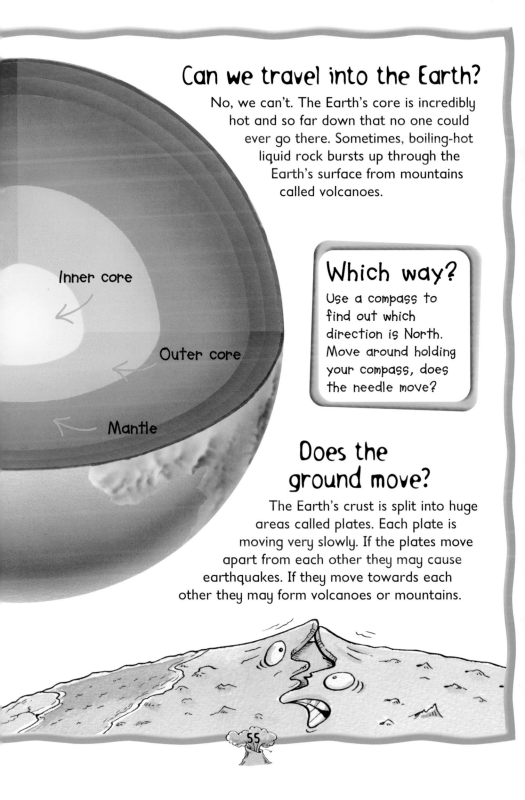

Can we travel into the Earth?

No, we can't. The Earth's core is incredibly hot and so far down that no one could ever go there. Sometimes, boiling-hot liquid rock bursts up through the Earth's surface from mountains called volcanoes.

Inner core

Outer core

Mantle

Which way?

Use a compass to find out which direction is North. Move around holding your compass, does the needle move?

Does the ground move?

The Earth's crust is split into huge areas called plates. Each plate is moving very slowly. If the plates move apart from each other they may cause earthquakes. If they move towards each other they may form volcanoes or mountains.

What is a fossil?

A trilobite was an ancient sea creature

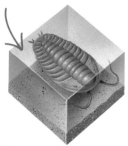

A fossil was once a living thing that has now turned to stone. By studying fossils, scientists can learn more about the past and how animals, such as dinosaurs, used to live.

Scientists digging up and studying fossils

How is a fossil made?

It takes millions of years to make a fossil. When an animal dies, it may be buried by sand. The soft parts of its body rot away, leaving just bones, teeth or shells. These slowly turn to rock and a fossil has formed.

Find

Look for rocks in your garden. They may be so old dinosaurs could have trodden on them.

1. The trilobite dies

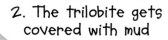

2. The trilobite gets covered with mud

3. The mud turns to stone

House of stones!

In Turkey, some people live in caves. These huge cone-shaped rocks stay very cool in the hot weather.

4. The fossil forms inside the stone

Why do rocks crumble?

When a rock is warmed up by the Sun it gets a little bigger. When it cools down, the rock shrinks to its original size. If this process happens to a rock too often, it starts to crumble away.

What is a volcano?

A volcano is a mountain that sometimes shoots hot, liquid rock out of its top. Deep inside a volcano is an area called a magma chamber. This is filled with liquid rock. If pressure builds up in the chamber, the volcano may explode, and liquid rock will shoot out of the top.

Liquid rock

Erupting volcano

Magma chamber

What is a range?

A range is the name for a group of mountains. The biggest ranges are the Alps in Europe, the Andes in South America, the Rockies in North America and the highest of all – the Himalayas in Asia.

How are mountains made?

One way that mountains are formed is when the Earth's plates crash together. The crust at the edge of the plates slowly crumples and folds. Over millions of years this pushes up mountains. The Himalayan Mountains in Asia were made this way.

Mountain range is pushed up

Layer on layer

When a volcano erupts, the hot lava cools and forms a rocky layer. With each new eruption, another layer is added and the volcano gets bigger.

Why are there earthquakes?

Earthquakes happen when the plates in the Earth's crust move apart suddenly, or rub together. They start deep underground in an area called the focus. The land above the focus is shaken violently. The worst part of the earthquake happens above the focus, in an area called the epicentre.

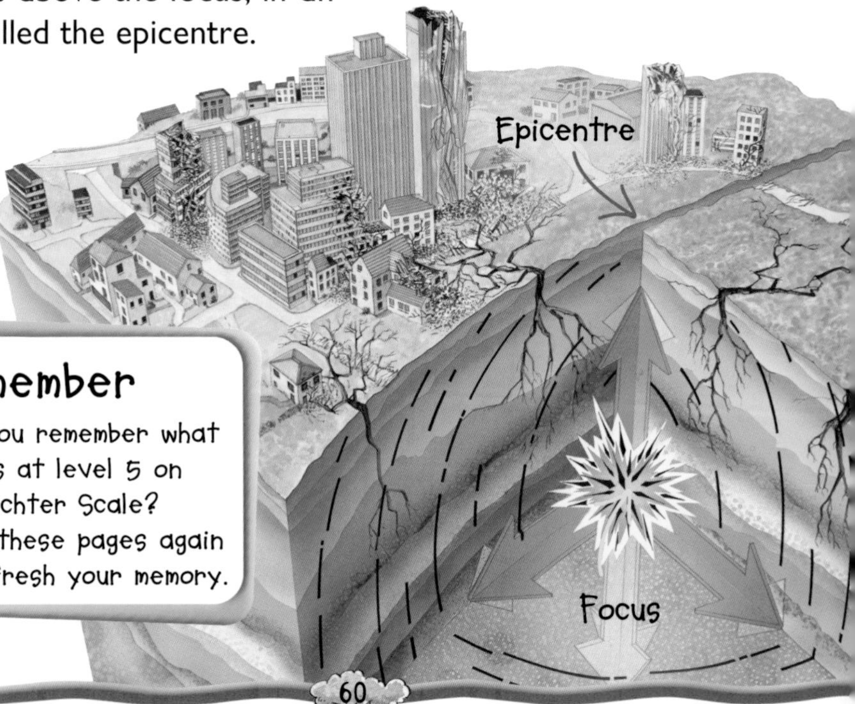

Epicentre

Focus

Remember

Can you remember what breaks at level 5 on the Richter Scale? Read these pages again to refresh your memory.

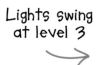

Lights swing at level 3

Windows break at level 5

Bridges and buildings collapse at level 7

What is The Richter Scale?

The Richter Scale measures the strength of an earthquake. It starts at number one and goes up to number eight. The higher the number, the more powerful and destructive the earthquake.

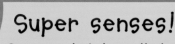

Super senses!

Some people believe that animals can sense when an earthquake is about to happen!

Can earthquakes start fires?

Yes, a powerful earthquake can cause fires. In 1906, a huge earthquake in San Francisco, USA caused lots of fires. The fires burnt down most of the city and the people who lived there became homeless.

What is a glacier?

Glaciers are huge rivers of ice found near the tops of mountains. Snow falls on the mountain and becomes squashed to make ice. The ice forms a glacier that slowly moves down the mountainside until it melts.

Moving glacier

Fancy flakes!

Snowflakes are made of millions of tiny crystals. No two snowflakes are the same because the crystals make millions of different shapes.

Melted ice

Can ice be fun?

Yes, it can! Many people go ice skating and they wear special boots with blades on them called ice skates. Figure skaters are skilled athletes who compete to win prizes.

What is an iceberg?

Icebergs are big chunks of ice that have broken off glaciers and drifted into the sea. Only a small part of the iceberg can be seen above the water. The main part of the iceberg is hidden under the water.

Iceberg

Look

Next time it snows, put some gloves on and let the snowflakes fall into your hand. Can you see crystals?

Where do rivers flow to?

Rivers flow to the sea or into lakes. They start off as small streams in hills and mountains. The streams flow downhill, getting bigger and wider. The place where a river meets the sea, or flows into a lake, is called the river mouth.

Oxbow lake

River mouth

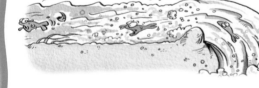

Why are there waterfalls?

Waterfalls are made when water wears down rocks to make a cliff face. The water then falls over the edge into a deep pool called a plunge pool. Waterfalls may only be a few centimetres high, or several hundred metres high!

Discover

Try to find out the name of the highest waterfall in the world. Where is it?

A river begins in the mountains

Meander

Risky business!

Salmon are a type of fish. Every year, fishermen try to catch them as they swim back to the river they were born in to have their babies.

What is a lake?

A lake is a big area of water that is surrounded by land. Some lakes are so big that they are called inland seas. Most lake water is fresh rather than salty. The biggest lake in the world is the Caspian Sea in Asia.

Lake

How are caves made?

When rain falls on rock, it can make caves. Rainwater mixes with a gas in the air called carbon dioxide. This makes a strong acid. This acid can attack the rock and make it disappear. Underground, the rainwater makes caves in which streams and lakes can be found.

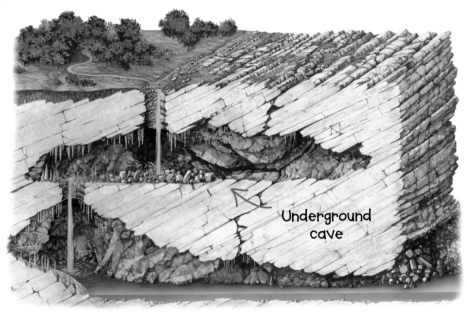

Underground cave

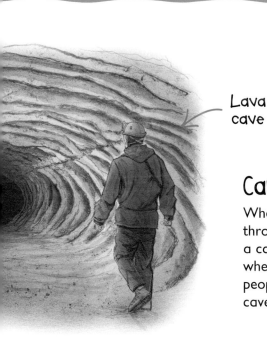

Lava cave

Can lava make caves?

When a volcano erupts and lava flows through the mountain, it can carve out a cave. A long time after the eruption, when the volcano is no longer active, people can walk through this lava cave without having to bend down.

What is a stalactite?

Rocky spikes that hang from cave ceilings are called stalactites. When water drips from the cave ceiling, it leaves tiny amounts of a rocky substance behind. Very slowly, over a long period of time, this grows into a stalactite.

Super spiky!

Stalagmites grow up from the cave floor. Dripping water leaves a rocky substance that grows into a rocky spike.

Is there water in the desert?

Yes there is. Deserts sometimes get rain. This rainwater seeps into the sand and collects in rock. The water then builds up and forms a pool called an oasis. Plants grow around the oasis and animals visit the pool to drink.

Oasis

What are grasslands?

Grasslands are found when there is too much rain for a desert but not enough rain for a forest. Large numbers of animals can be found living and feeding on grasslands, including zebras, antelopes and lions.

Draw

Create a picture of a camel crossing a desert — don't forget to include its wide feet!

Big feet!

Camels have wide feet that stop them sinking into the sand. They can also store water in their bodies for a long time.

Rainforest

What is a rainforest?

In hot places, such as South America, grow areas of thick, green forest. These are rainforests, and they are home to many amazing plants and animals. Rainforests have rainy weather all year round.

69

Where does rain come from?

Rain comes from the ocean! Water moves between the ocean, air and land in a water cycle. A fine mist of water rises into the air from the ocean and from plants. This fine mist then forms clouds. Water can fall from the clouds as rain.

Water falls from clouds as rain

Water cycle

Stormy weather!

Every day there are more than 45,000 thunderstorms on the Earth! Thunderstorms are most common in tropical places, such as Indonesia.

How does a tornado start?

A tornado is the fastest wind on Earth. Tornadoes start over very hot ground. Here, warm air rises quickly and makes a spinning funnel. This funnel acts like a vacuum cleaner, destroying buildings and lifting cars and lorries off the ground.

Tornado

A fine mist of water rises from the ocean

Do storms have eyes?

Yes, storms do have eyes! A hurricane is a very dangerous storm. The centre of a hurricane is called the eye and here it is completely still. However, the rest of the storm can reach speeds of up to 300 kilometres an hour.

Which star keeps us warm?

The Sun does. It is a star like all the others in the night sky, but it is much closer to Earth. The Sun is a giant ball of hot, glowing gas and it gives off heat that keeps the Earth warm. It also gives us light.

Hot hot hot!

The Sun's surface is so hot that it would melt a metal spacecraft flying near it! It is 15 times hotter than boiling water.

When is it night time during the day?

Sometimes the Sun, the Earth and the Moon all line up in space. When this happens, the Moon's shadow falls on the Earth, making it dark even if it's daytime. This is called an eclipse.

Eclipse

Sunspot

Why is the Sun spotty?

Some parts of the Sun's surface are cooler than the rest of it. These cooler parts appear darker than the rest of the Sun, like spots on its surface. They are called sunspots.

Remember
Never look straight at the Sun. Your eyes could be badly damaged.

73

Is Earth the only planet near the Sun?

There are seven other planets near the Sun. Mercury and Venus are nearer to the Sun than the Earth is. The other planets are further away. All the planets move around the Sun in huge circles. The Sun and its family of planets is called the Solar System.

Saturn

Uranus

Neptune

Pluto
(dwarf planet)

Draw

Can you draw a picture of all the planets? You could copy the pictures on this page.

74

Do other planets have moons?

Earth is not the only planet with a moon. Mars has two moons. Jupiter and Saturn have more than 30 moons each. Venus and Mercury are the only planets with no moons.

The Sun

Mercury

The Moon

Venus

Mars

Earth

Jupiter

What are the other planets like?

Mercury, Venus and Mars are rocky planets, like the Earth. They have solid surfaces. Jupiter, Saturn, Uranus and Neptune are balls of gas and liquid. They are much bigger than the rocky planets. Pluto is a dwarf planet.

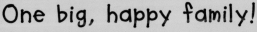

One big, happy family!

There are millions of smaller members in the Sun's family. Tiny specks of dust speed between the planets along with chunks of rock called asteroids.

What is inside the Earth?

There are layers of hot rock inside the Earth. We live on the Earth's surface where the rock is solid. Beneath the surface, the rock is hot. In some places, it has melted. This melted rock may leak from a volcano.

Crust

Mantle

Inner core

Outer core

Living it up!

Earth is the only planet with water on its surface. This means that people, plants and animals can live here. No life has yet been found on other planets.

New Moon

Crescent
Moon

First quarter
Moon

Gibbous
Moon

Full Moon

Why does the Moon change shape?

The Sun lights up one side of the Moon. The other side is dark. As the Moon circles the Earth, we see different parts of the lit side. This is why the Moon seems to change shape.

The Moon

Why do we have day and night?

The Earth spins round once every day. When the part you live on faces the Sun, it is daytime. When this part faces away from the Sun, the sunlight can't reach you. Then it is night time.

Look

Look at the picture of the Moon. The circles are called craters. They were made by lumps of rock smashing into the Moon's surface.

77

What is the hottest planet?

Venus is the hottest planet in the Solar System. Its surface is hotter than the inside of an oven. Venus is covered in a blanket of thick, yellow gas. The gases trap heat from the Sun but don't let it escape. This means that Venus can't cool down.

Back in a year!

Nobody has ever been to Mars. It is so far away that it would take a spacecraft six months to get there. It would take another six months to get home again!

Venus

Why is Mars called the red planet?

Mars looks red because it is covered with red rocks and red dust, the colour of rust. Sometimes, winds pick up the dust and make swirling dust storms. In 1971 dust storms covered the whole planet. The surface completely disappeared from view!

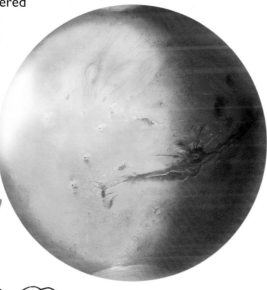

Mars

Which planet has the biggest volcano?

Mars has the biggest volcano. It is called Olympus Mons and it is three times higher than Mount Everest, the highest mountain on Earth. Olympus Mons has gently sloping sides, like an upside-down plate. Mars has many other volcanoes, too. There are also giant canyons and craters.

Discover

Try looking for Venus in the night sky. It looks like a bright star in the early morning or evening.

Does Pluto have its own moon?

Yes, it does. Pluto, a dwarf planet, has its own moon called Charon. Charon is half the size of Pluto and was discovered by scientists in 1978. It takes Charon six and a half Earth days to orbit around Pluto.

Charon, Pluto's moon

Pluto

Pluto's surface

Why does Mercury look like the Moon?

Mercury looks a bit like our Moon. It is covered in dents called craters. These were made when rocks crashed into the surface. There is no wind or rain on Mercury, or the Moon, to wear away the craters.

Sun trap!

Mercury is very close to the Sun. It gets much hotter there than on Earth. If you travelled to Mercury, you would need a special spacesuit and shoes to protect you from the heat.

⟵ Mercury

Think

Pluto is really cold. Can you think why?

Which planet is baking hot and freezing cold?

Mercury is hot and cold. It spins very slowly. The side that faces the Sun is baked until it is hotter than the inside of an oven. When this side faces away from the Sun, it cools down until it is colder than a freezer.

What is the biggest planet?

Jupiter is the biggest planet. It is 11 times as wide as the Earth. All the other planets in the Solar System would fit inside it! Jupiter is covered in swirls of red and orange gas. These are giant storms.

Giant storm

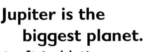

Jupiter

Moon pizza!

Io is one of Jupiter's moons. It is covered in yellow and orange blotches. Io looks like a pizza in space! The blotches are made by hot liquid that comes out of volcanoes.

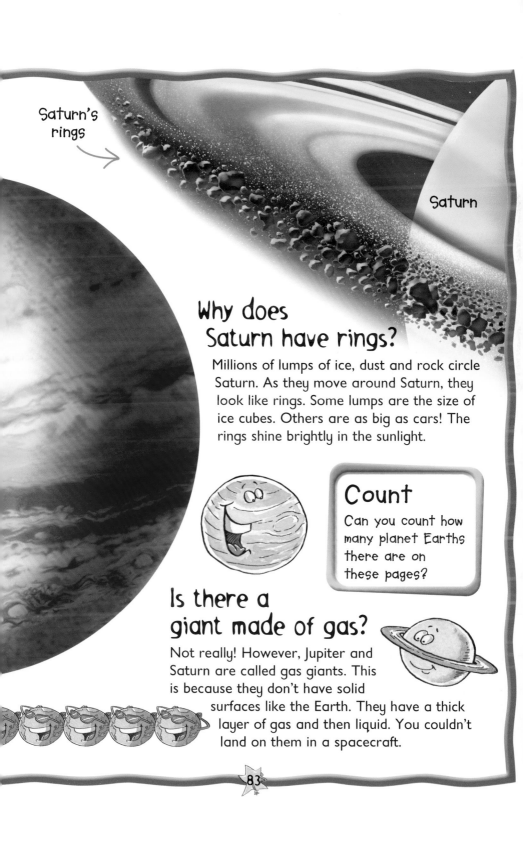

Saturn's rings

Saturn

Why does Saturn have rings?

Millions of lumps of ice, dust and rock circle Saturn. As they move around Saturn, they look like rings. Some lumps are the size of ice cubes. Others are as big as cars! The rings shine brightly in the sunlight.

Count

Can you count how many planet Earths there are on these pages?

Is there a giant made of gas?

Not really! However, Jupiter and Saturn are called gas giants. This is because they don't have solid surfaces like the Earth. They have a thick layer of gas and then liquid. You couldn't land on them in a spacecraft.

Which planet rolls around?

Uranus is different to the other planets. Most planets are almost upright. They spin as they move around the Sun. Uranus is tipped right over on its side. This planet spins, too, but it looks as though it is rolling around!

New new moons!

Astronomers (scientists that study space) keep finding new moons around Uranus. They have found 27 so far. There are four big moons and lots of small ones. But there may be more!

Uranus

Why does Neptune look so blue?

Neptune is covered in bright blue clouds. Sometimes there are streaky, icy white clouds, too. One white cloud is called The Scooter because it scoots around Neptune at high speed. There is also a giant storm called the Great Dark Spot.

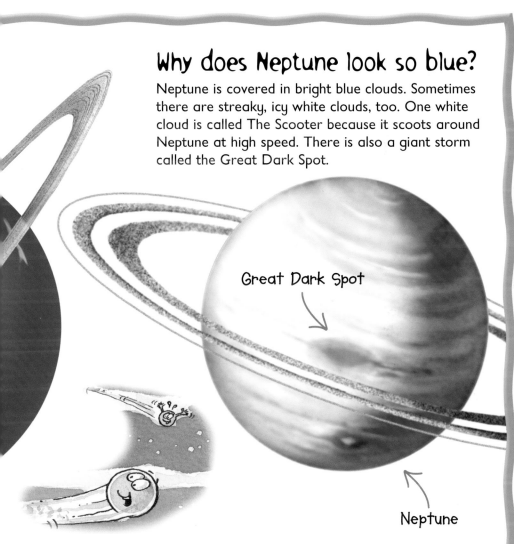

Great Dark Spot

Neptune

Why do Neptune and Pluto swap places?

Most of the planets move around the Sun in huge circles. Pluto's circle is a bit squashed. This means that it is sometimes closer to the Sun than Neptune. Then it is Neptune's turn to be the planet that is furthest from the Sun!

Remember

Uranus and Neptune have rings. Which other two planets have rings, too?

What is the Milky Way?

The stars in space are in huge groups called galaxies. Our galaxy is called the Milky Way. All the stars in the night sky are in the Milky Way. There are so many that you couldn't count them all in your whole lifetime!

Can galaxies crash?

Sometimes two galaxies crash into each other. But there is no giant bump. This is because galaxies are mostly made of empty space! The stars just go past each other. Galaxies can pull each other out of shape.

Count

Look at the pictures on these pages. How many different shapes of galaxies can you find?

The Milky Way

Elliptical galaxy

Do galaxies have arms?

Some galaxies have arms that curl in a spiral, like the Milky Way. Other galaxies, called elliptical galaxies, have a round, squashed shape. Many galaxies have no shape and are called irregular galaxies.

Irregular galaxy

Spiral galaxy

Great galaxies!

There are thousands of millions of galaxies in space. Some are much smaller than the Milky Way. Others are much larger. They all contain too many stars to count!

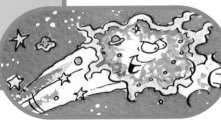

How does a shuttle get into space?

Booster rocket

Tower

A shuttle blasts into space like a big rocket. It has rocket motors in its tail. They get fuel from a giant fuel tank. There are two booster rockets, too. The fuel tank and the booster rockets fall off before the shuttle reaches space.

US

Rocket power!

Rockets are filled with fuel. The fuel burns in the rocket motor to make hot gases. The gases rush out of the motor and push the rocket upwards.

Fuel tank

Space shuttle

Rocket motors

How fast do rockets go?

Very, very fast indeed! After blasting off, a rocket goes faster and faster and higher and higher. When it reaches space, it is going 30 times faster than a jumbo jet. If a rocket went slower than this it would fall back to Earth.

Rocket

Make

Blow up a balloon and then let it go. The air rushes out and pushes the balloon along, like a simple rocket.

When is a shuttle like a glider?

When a shuttle travels back to Earth it slows down. Then it begins to fall. It does not use its motors to fly down. Instead, it flies like a giant glider. The shuttle lands on a long runway and uses a parachute to slow to a stop.

Why do astronauts float in space?

When things are in space they don't have any weight. This means everything floats. So do astronauts! This makes them feel sick, too. In a spacecraft everything is fixed down to stop it floating away. Astronauts have footholds and handholds to grab onto.

All packed?

Astronauts must take everything they need into space. In space there is no air, water or food. All of these things have to be packed into the spacecraft and taken into space.

Astronaut   Sleeping bag

Where do astronauts go to sleep?

Astronauts sleep in sleeping bags. The bags are fixed to the wall inside a spacecraft. They keep astronauts warm and stop them floating about while they sleep! A special shower lets the astronauts wash without drops of water floating everywhere.

Why do astronauts wear spacesuits?

Space is a dangerous place. Spacesuits protect astronauts when they go outside their spacecraft. There is no air in space. So a spacesuit has a supply of air for the astronaut to breathe. The suit also stops an astronaut from getting too hot or too cold.

Remember
Can you remember why astronauts have to carry air with them in space?

Are there robots in space?

There are robot spacecraft, called probes, in space. They have visited all the planets. Some probes travel around the planets. They send photographs and other information back to Earth. Other probes land on a planet to take a closer look.

Snap happy!

A probe called *Voyager 2* was the first to visit Uranus and Neptune. It took photographs of the planets and sent them back to Earth.

Viking probe on Mars

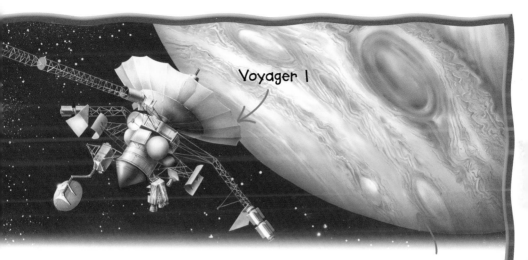

Voyager 1

Jupiter

Which probe has travelled the furthest?

A probe called *Voyager 1* was launched from Earth in 1977. It visited Jupiter in 1979 and then Saturn in 1980. Then it kept going, out of the Solar System. *Voyager 1* is now 14 thousand million kilometres from Earth!

Draw

Try designing your own robot explorer. You can take some ideas from these pages.

Sojourner

Have probes been to Mars?

More probes have been to Mars than any other planet. In 1997 a probe called Pathfinder landed on Mars. Inside Pathfinder was a tiny robot vehicle, called *Sojourner*. Scientists steered it using remote control. It investigated the soil and rocks on Mars.

Index